A LITTLE BOOK OF KENT

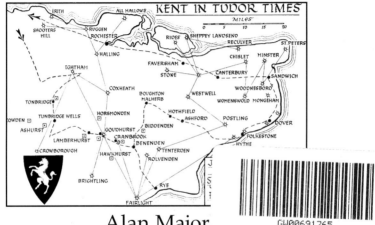

Alan Major
Illustrations by the a

S.B. Publications

By the same author
A New Dictionary of Kent Dialect, Meresborough Books 1981
Who's Buried Where in Kent, Meresborough Books 1990
Hidden Kent, Countryside Books 1994
Cherries in the Rise, 1997   *Goldings, Napoleons and Romneys*, 1999
The Kentish Lights, 2000   *A Kent Quiz Book*, 2000
Kentish As She Wus Spoke, 2001
All published by S. B. Publications

First published in 2002 by S. B. Publications
19 Grove Road, Seaford, East Sussex. Tel: 01323 893498

ISBN 1 85770 262 X

Designed and typeset by CGB editorial services, Lewes. Tel: 01273 476622
Printed by Pageturn Ltd, East Sussex, BN3 7EG. Tel: 01273 821500

CONTENTS

Introduction

What makes Kent special? Everyone will have his or her own answers to this question, depending on whether they are Kent born and bred, or a 'foreigner' from another county and retaining an allegiance to it. I have traced my ancestry in Kent back via my maternal grandparents, the Nortons, to the villages of Pluckley, Egerton, Great Chart and Bethersden in the late sixteenth century so my enthusiasm for the county must be inborn.

In the following pages I hope to convey, in words and with pictures, the feel of Kent in its varying aspects – and include some little-known and fascinating facts about it. Although there has been much modern development unspoilt areas do survive where one can walk in the footsteps of those who went before and see the county through their eyes.

This book is dedicated to all the Men and Women of Kent and Kentish Men and Women loyal to the county of their birth for whatever reason and to all those incomers who wisely decided that this is where they must live.

Alan Major, Canterbury
October 2002

Kent Claims to Fame

In 1533 cherries were cultivated commercially for the first time in Kent by Richard Harris, Henry VIII's 'gardener-fruiterer' on the 105 acres of the Brennet at Teynham.

Guglielmo Marconi, the Italian pioneer of wireless telegraphy, obtained permission from Trinity House, to install his Wireless Telegraph and Signal Company's equipment in a room in the engine house of South Foreland lighthouse to experiment with achieving ship-to-shore communications.

On 24 December 1898, he successfully established the first over-the-sea communication from the lighthouse to the East Goodwin lightship, which was also equipped with wireless apparatus and anchored 12 miles distant on the east side of the Goodwin Sands.

A plaque on a wall of Canterbury West railway station reads:

> NEAR HERE WAS THE TERMINUS OF THE CANTERBURY & WHITSTABLE RAILWAY, 1830 (GEORGE STEPHENSON, ENGINEER). THE WORLD'S FIRST RAILWAY SEASON TICKETS WERE ISSUED HERE 1834.

This railway opened on 3 May 1830 and was the first of its kind in the south of England.

The Romney, Hythe and Dymchurch Light Railway was the first and smallest public railway in Britain, some say in the world. It was the brainchild of Captain John Howey who, as a small boy, not only wanted to be an engine driver but to build his own railway. He chose the Romney Marsh area to do so because it needed a railway but it was not suitable for a full-size one. The engines on the RHDR are one third full size and are modelled on various famous locomotives.

Construction work between Hythe and New Romney began in 1926 and the railway opened the following year. The line was extended in 1928 to the Pilot Inn and in 1929 to Dungeness lighthouse.

The first British aircraft factory and first airfield in England was set up on 400 acres of the former golf course at Leysdown, Sheppey in 1909 by Short Brothers, engineers to the Aero Club, later the Royal Aero Club. However, there were land drainage problems at Leysdown so in 1910 the Aero Club moved its flying ground and the Short brothers their factory to the former Stonepitts Farm at Eastchurch.

A statue of C S Rolls on the sea front at Dover.

Before the First World War there was more flying of powered aircraft from Sheppey than anywhere else in Britain. Many notable people flew from Eastchurch, among them Lord Brabazon of Tara, holder of the first pilot's licence; Sir Thomas Sopwith who built the Sopwith Camel fighter plane; Sir Winston Churchill and Charles Stewart Rolls of Rolls-Royce fame, the first to cross the Channel and return in a single flight.

✳ ✳ ✳

8

The first cross-Channel flight by aeroplane was made by Louis Bleriot on 25 July 1909. He landed at Northfall Meadow, near Dover Castle. The site is marked by a granite replica of his monoplane.

Percy Pilcher, the aeronautical pioneer, built his gliders near Lower Austin and Upper Austin farms, Eynsford, and tested them in the area of Magpie Bottom. With his Hawk glider, which weighed only 50 lbs, he flew 250 yards from one hilltop to another in 1897.

Pilcher's ambition was to be the first man to make a powered flight and, for this purpose, designed a 4hp engine to propel his craft. However, before it was built and could be tested the thirty-three year old airman was persuaded to give a gliding exhibition to members of the Aeronautical Society at Stanford Park, Rugby, on 30 September 1899.

It was a gusty, rainy day and when his Hawk glider reached a height of 30ft its tail collapsed and it crashed. Pilcher was badly injured and died two days later, so tragically becoming the first Briton to be killed in a gliding accident.

Near the west door of St Leonards church at Hythe is the grave of coach-maker Lionel Lukin, (1742-1834) inventor of the first successful lifeboat.

Part of the inscription on the headstone reads:

THIS LIONEL LUKIN WAS THE FIRST WHO BUILT A LIFE BOAT AND WAS THE ORIGINAL INVENTOR OF THAT PRINCIPLE OF SAFETY BY WHICH MANY LIVES AND MUCH PROPERTY HAVE BEEN PRESERVED FROM SHIPWRECK AND HE OBTAINED FOR IT THE KING'S PATENT IN THE YEAR 1785.

The first motor show to be held in England, the Horseless Carriage Exhibition, was at Tunbridge Wells Agricultural Society's showground on 15 October 1895. It was open from 3pm to 5pm and admission was one shilling (5p).

The show was organised by the Mayor of Tunbridge Wells, Sir David Salomons of Broomhill, Southborough,

A Type 25 Peugeot three quarter coupe was brought from France for the show.

and he went to Paris and brought back an elegant new three-quarter coupe Peugeot. He also persuaded friends to exhibit their vehicles and these included a Panhard with a Daimler engine, a de Dion motor tricycle, a de Dion and Bouton 'Steam Horse' and a Panhard and Levassor fire engine. Several thousands came to the show, probably quite unaware that they were seeing motoring history in the making.

The first paper mill in Kent was founded by Sir John Spielman at Dartford in 1588, after obtaining a licence to manufacture paper from Elizabeth I. He was a German from Landau and his surname – spiel, which is modern slang for salesman's patter from the German, play, or game - translated into joker or jester, someone who plays games or tricks. As a watermark on his papers he used a design of a jester's cap, hence the origin of 'foolscap', for the size of paper he produced.

William Harvey, an English physician, born at Folkestone in 1578, was the first to discover the circulation of the blood. He wrote of his discoveries and theories in *On the Movement of the Heart and Blood in Animals,* published in Amsterdam in 1628. Pictured right is the statue of him holding a heart, which stands on the Leas. More than 3,000 members of the medical profession subscribed to the Harvey memorial window which is in St Mary and St Eanswith church, Folkestone.

It was in 1886, when he was living at Tower House, Orpington, that William Cook bred and first exhibited his Black Orpington chickens. He followed them up with his equally successful White Orpingtons in 1888. When he moved in 1890 to Walden Manor, St Mary Cray, he renamed the property Orpington House and from there introduced the world-famous Buff Orpington in 1894 and in 1897 the Diamond Jubilee Orpington.

A Buff Orpington hen and cockerel.

Queen Victoria was graciously pleased to accept a number of them.

William Cook's daughters shared their father's interest in breeding poultry, Elizabeth producing the Cuckoo Orpington and Blue Orpington chickens and Catherine breeding Blue Orpington and Buff Orpington ducks and the Speckled Orpington chickens.

Market gardening, a trade new to this country, was brought to the flat, fertile soil around Sandwich by Dutch gardeners, fleeing from religious and political persecution in the Low Countries. In 1560 Elizabeth I granted them permission, and means, to established this trade. Among the crops they produced, and sent to local and London markets, was the first celery cultivated in England. Several areas and farms around Sandwich are still known by the Dutch names of poulder, polder and felderland.

On 21 June, 1854, while serving as mate on HMS *Hecla* in the Baltic during the Crimean War, 20 year old Charles Davis Lucas picked up a live shell that landed on the deck and threw it overboard where it exploded. The shell was one with a short time fuse set to explode a few seconds after impact and his prompt action saved the lives of many of the crew and possibly also saved the ship. For this brave act he was awarded the first Victoria Cross and received the medal with its simple inscription 'For Valour' personally from Queen Victoria on 26 June 1857. Lucas, who died in 1914, is buried in St Laurence's churchyard, Mereworth.

Benjamin Harrison (1837-1921), a grocer by trade and an archaeologist by inclination, was one of the first in England to realise the shaped flints he found on Oldbury Hill on the North Downs were artefacts made and used by Stone Age men.

Examples of the Stone Age flint arrowheads found on Oldbury Hill.

One of these worked flints is mounted above a memorial tablet to him in St Peter's church, Ightham. He was buried in the churchyard, north-west of the church tower, and the inscription on his gravestone concludes with a quotation from Shakespeare's *As You Like It*:

HE FOUND IN LIFE 'BOOKS IN THE RUNNING BROOKS,
SERMONS IN STONES AND
GOOD IN EVERYTHING.'

Beneath an insignificant stone slab by the north wall of St Mary's church at Bishopsbourne, is buried a former rector of the parish, the Reverend

Joseph Bancroft Reade (1801-1870). Forgotten now, he was one of the principal pioneers in the field of photography and, in addition, an inventor of a number of improvements in the use of a microscope and camera.

He studied the microscopic structure of Kent chalk and in 1838 wrote *a* paper on *Some New Organic Remains in Flint and Chalk,* which had the first published illustrations of prehistoric marine organisms.

His most important discovery, however, was that an infusion of oak galls made photographic paper more sensitive and that it was possible to develop an image by using gallic acid.

Joseph Reade's 'insignificant grave slab'.

The first elephant to be seen in England was landed on The Quay, Sandwich, in 1255. It was a gift to Henry III for his zoo in the Tower of London from the King of France.

It is difficult to understand why the elephant was not taken directly to London by boat rather than being landed here. Perhaps the Channel crossing had been rough and it was suffering from sea-sickness.

Whatever the reason, it was decided to walk the elephant to the Tower. It arrived safely, after being charged by a bull at Wingham. The elephant killed the bull.

The Spirit of Kent

An eighteenth century engraving of Dover castle and the white cliffs.

'If we survey, with critical acumen, the whole surface of England, there is no portion of its territory more abundant, or more calculated to captivate the eye, than the county of Kent. In whatsoever direction we proceed, the same pleasing diversified scenery presents itself, and, on attaining an eminence, no expansive view can be found chequered with more enchanting objects.'

William H Ireland, writing in England's Topographer or A New and Complete History of the County of Kent, *published in 1828.*

'This is what the people of Kent call the Garden of England. It is a district of meadows, cornfields, hop gardens and orchards of apples, pears, cherries and filberts, with very little, if any land which cannot, with propriety, be called good . . . From Maidstone to this place [Mereworth] is about seven miles and these are the finest seven miles I have ever seen in England or anywhere else.'

William Cobbett, in his Rural Rides, *1830. And of Chatham he wrote:*

'Here, at between sixteen and seventeen I enlisted for a soldier. On looking up towards the fortifications and the barracks, how many recollections crowded into my mind . . . One thing I will say for young women of these towns [Rochester, Chatham, Brompton] and that is that I always found those of them that I had the great happiness to be acquainted with, evince a sincere desire to do their best to smooth the inequalities of life and to give us, 'brave fellows', as often as they could, strong beer, when their churlish masters or fathers or husbands would have drenched us to death with small.'

'I love Kent although I was born in Oxfordshire. I was brought up by an old nurse, who was born at Chatham, always to think of Kent as the Garden of England. Now my home is in Kent and I am delighted to see around me so many of the gardeners'.

Sir Winston Churchill at the opening of the Kent County Agricultural Show, at Mote Park, Maidstone, on 14 July 1948.

'I have many happy recollections connected with Kent and am scarcely less interested in it than if I had been a Kentish man bred and born and had resided in the county all my life.

Charles Dickens, in a letter to a friend from his home at Gad's Hill.

'I passed the end of May and all June in Kent not disagreeably, the country is all a garden, gay, rich and fruitful and (from the rainy season) had preserved, till I left it, all that emerald verdure which commonly one only sees for the first fortnight of the spring. In the west part of it, from every eminence, the eye catches some long winding reach of the Thames or Medway . . . in the east the sea breaks in upon you and mixes its white transient sails and glittering blue expanse with the deeper and brighter greens of the woods and corn.'

The poet, Thomas Gray of Elegy fame, writing to a friend, the Reverend Nicholas Norton, in 1766.

After a visit to Rochester, Samuel Pepys wrote in his diary on 30 June 1667:

Then into the fields, a fine walk, and into the cherry garden, where we had them fresh gathered, and here met with a young, plain, silly shop-keeper, and his wife, a pretty young woman. We talked and eat cherries together and then to walk in the fields till it was late and did kiss her.

Charles Darwin, after moving from London into Down House, Downe, (pictured right) in 1842, wrote to his sister, Catherine, about the countryside around his home:

The charm of the place to me is that almost every field is intersected by one or more footpaths. I never saw so many walks in any other county. It is really surprising to think London is only 16 miles off . . .'

When he was editor of the *Cornhill Magazine* in 1860 the novelist William Makepeace Thackeray lived in Tunbridge Wells – at Rock Villa, 85 London

Road, on the edge of the Common and the corner of Mount Ephraim Road. He described the area to his readers:

. . . I stroll over the Common and survey the beautiful purple hills around, twinkling with a thousand bright villas, which have sprung up over this charming ground since I first saw it. What an admirable scene of peace and plenty: What a delicious air breathes over the heath, blows the cloud shadows across it and murmurs through the full-clad trees. Can the world show a land, fairer, richer, more cheerful?

Kent in Verse

The 'Dymchurch Wall' of John Davidson's poem, **In Romney Marsh.**

From
POLYOLBION

O famous Kent
What county hath this isle that can compare with thee?
That hath within thyself as much as thou canst wish,
Thy rabbits, venison, fruits, thy sorts of fowl and fish,
As with what strength comports thy hay, thy corn, thy wood,
Nor anything doth want that anywhere is good.
MICHAEL DRAYTON (1563-1631)

A SONG OF KENT
Oh, some love Sussex by the sea,
And others sing of Devon,
But still to me the Kentish land
Is fairest under Heaven.

I love her fruit trees white with bloom
In cherry orchard time,
Her lovely fields with hop-bines clad
When summer's at the prime.

What noble ruins Kent can show!
What memories of her race
Are scattered over her hills and dales
In many an ancient place!

Oh! Men of Kent! and Kentish Men!
Right happy may you be,
Because of all broad England's shires
The fairest falls to thee.

MARGARET OWEN

IN ROMNEY MARSH

As I went down to Dymchurch Wall,
I heard the South sing o'er the land;
I saw the yellow sunlight fall
On knolls where Norman churches stand.

And ringing shrilly, taut and lithe,
Within the wind a core of sound,
The wire from Romney town to Hythe
Alone its airy journey wound.

A veil of purple vapour flowed
And trailed its fringe along the Straits;
The upper air like sapphire glowed
And roses filled Heaven's central gates.

Masts in the offing wagged their tops;
The swinging waves peal'd on the shore;

The saffron beach, all diamond drops
And beads of surge, prolonged the roar.

As I came up from Dymchurch Wall,
I saw above the Downs' low crest
The crimson bands of sunset fall
Flicker and fade from out the west.

Night sank: like flakes of silver fire
The stars in one great shower came down;
Shrill blew the wind and shrill the wire
Rang out from Hythe to Romney town.

The darkly shining salt sea drops
Streamed as the waves clashed on the shore
The beach, with all its organ stops
Pealing again, prolonged the roar.

JOHN DAVIDSON (1857-1909)

TRADITIONAL KENTISH RHYME

Rye, Romney and Hythe, for wealth without health,
The Downs for health with poverty:
But you shall find both health and wealth
From Foreland Head to Knole and Lee.

THE WOOING SONG OF A YEOMAN OF KENT'S SONNE
An old Kentish song, date unknown

Ich am my vather's eldest sonne
My mouther eke doth love me well:
For ich can bravely clout my shoone
And ich full well can ring a bell.

My vather he gave me a hogge,
My mouther she gave me a zow;

Ich have a good-vather dwells there by
And he on me bestowed a plough.

One time ich gave thee a paper of pins
Anoder time a taudry lace;
And if thou wilt not grant me love
In truth ich die bevore thy vace.

Ich have been twice our Whitson lord,
Ich have had ladies many vare;
And eke thou hast my heart in hold,
And in my minde zeems passing rare.

Ich will put on my best white sloppe
And ich will wear my yellow hose;
And on my head a good gray hat
And in't ich sticke a lovely rose.

OLD KENTISH SONG

In war and debate
He saved the state;
He made the haughty foe to bow,
And when all was done, came back to the plough,
Like a right good Kentish yeoman.

THE MARGATE HOY

So soon as we landed on this pretty spot,
As 'twere a fresh dainty from town, piping hot
There came all about us, with bows to the ground,
From all the hotels in the neighbourhood round,
A set of such waiters, so frizzed and flour'd,
We seem with civility quite overpowered.
One snatched up the saddle-bags, bearing my best coat,
My yard and a half buckskins and fur-collared waistcoat;

Another my father's portmanteau and many
The pile of band-boxes of Mother and Nanny,
The maid followed after and carried her own
Little bundle containing a clean linen gown.
As thus in procession we went up the beach,
I thought it but proper to make a short speech.
Said I, 'Gentlemen – be so good as to say
If you're all going one, or a diff'erent way,
Because you see, Father, Mother and I
Would go to one House as we came in one Hoy.

Hoys were small coastal sailing ships that plied up and down the Thames from London carrying passengers and sundry goods to ports and resorts on the Kent and East Anglian coast. Before piers were built the passengers and their luggage were brought ashore in rowing boats or, if the hoy had come close inshore, on the backs of boatmen and others seeking a tip. On the beach to meet them would be touts for local hotels and inns. This was put into verse in 1791 by a 'Master Cockney' writing from Margate to a friend in London.

From
PENSHURST REVISITED

Near Penshurst Place the foursquare church tower stood
Proudly among the emerald crowns of trees,

Casting dark shadow; the church clock struck three.
Sweet prospect: Most blest village, dear to me,
Nestling in such luxuriant countryside
This June, this burning June :

I journey on and pass a darling cottage,
Minute, warm tinted, Kentish: pause, envying;
Press on again, find the half-shadowed road
Stretched like a ribbon flung to meet the hill;
Red oast-houses, by young, fast-climbing hops,
Slanting their witches hats against the sky.

A blackbird alights close, his tail at see-saw.
Now listen while he flutes: What ecstasy:
How rich his praise: That stream was rightly named,
For surely this sweet land is veriest Eden?

JOSEPH BRADDOCK

KENT SMUGGLERS

Some gallop this way and some gallop that,
Through Fordwich level, o'er Sandwich Flat . . .
Those in a hurry make for Sturry,
With Customs House officers close in their rear,
Down Rushbourne Lane and so by Westbere.
None of them stopping, but shooting and popping,
And many a Customs House bullet goes slap
Through many a three-gallon tub like a tap,
And the gin spurts out, and squirts all about;
And many a heart grew sad that day,
That so much liquor was so thrown away.

From *The Ingoldsby Legends* by
RICHARD HARRIS BARHAM (1788-1845)

Kent Buildings – and some piers

The church and timbered houses in The Square,
Chilham in 1905.

The weatherboarding of houses, cottages and barns was initially confined to Kent and the Kent-Sussex border area. The process used overlapping boards to cover brickwork exposed to the weather and throw off the rain.

The boards were painted – usually white – to make them waterproof or they were black tarred for the same purpose.

White weatherboarding on Rock Villa, 85 London Road, Tunbridge Wells, where William Makepeace Thackeray lived in 1860.

Troubles, it is said, always come in threes. It is hoped this will not apply in the case of the St Gregory and St Martin's church at Wye. In

1572 the wooden steeple was struck by lightning and set on fire. In March, 1686 the restored steeple collapsed when its four supporting pillars gave way, and demolished the entire east end of the church including the chancel and its transepts. These have not been rebuilt. The present low pinnacled tower was built on the south-east corner and an apsidal chancel constructed on the old tower site in 1701 with the result that some of the tombs, whose occupants probably paid to be inside in the warm and dry, are now outside in the churchyard.

The tower of St Mary's church, Upchurch, is capped by a shingled spire that has been variously described as 'a queer extinguisher-like spire, a candle-snuffer spire' and 'an almost grotesque two-piece spire'. It is half-square and half-octagonal in plan, the first tier having a pyramidical base with an octagonal second storey. The spire, formerly used as a navigation mark by shipping on the Medway,

had its top blown off in 1915 in the disastrous explosion that destroyed the minelayer *Princess Irene* off Port Victoria, Grain.

In 1560 the vicar of Upchurch was the Reverend Edmund Drake, father of Sir Francis, who, as a boy, is said to have learned his seamanship on the Medway hereabouts.

The riverside at Gravesend has three piers – Town Pier, Royal Terrace Pier and the West (Railway) Pier, all virtually equidistant. The Royal Terrace pier was built in 1842-43 by J B Redman and is one of the earliest examples

of the use of cast iron for the triglyph frieze and the Greek Doric columns on which the superstructure stands. It is believed to be the oldest surviving cast-iron pier in Europe but for a time in 1892 its future was uncertain. The pier, which was the pilot station for the port of London, was found to be in an unsafe condition and was closed. The following year, with the agreement of the Elder Brethren of Trinity House, the Channel and river pilots who used it purchased it for £12,000. The pier was restored, with almost 100ft being added to it riverwards, and was re-opened in June 1894.

From the landward entrance to the seaward side the present Deal pier is 882ft 9ins long – the exact length of the ill-fated liner *Titanic* – and was completed at a cost of £250, 000 in 1957. The pier prior to this one opened in 1864 and was more disastrously involved with a ship. In January, 1940, the Dutch vessel *Nora,* after hitting a mine and out of control, collided with and crashed through the pier. As an anti-invasion precaution, following the Dunkirk evacuation in the Second World War, the wrecked pier was removed.

Luddesdown Court, next to St Peter and St Paul church,Luddesdown, is believed to be the oldest house in continuous occupation not only in Kent but in England, its occupancy dating back to Odo, Bishop of Bayeux, William the Conqueror's half-brother.

It has features from Saxon, Norman and Tudor periods and it was built on the site of an early Iron Age hut, evidence of the existence of which was found under the chalk thrown out when the foundations for the Saxon manor house were excavated. There were red markings in the clay subsoil indicating an early dwelling had been destroyed by fire.

The first two bungalows in Britain were built at St Mildred's Bay, Westgate-on-Sea in 1867 by Sir Erasmus Wilson, son of a Dartford doctor. He patterned his single-storey homes on those of tea planters he had seen in Bengal and he called them 'Bengalos' for that reason.

Sir Erasmus, who financed the transportation by ship of Cleopatra's Needle from Egypt to the Thames Embankment, died at Westgate-on-Sea in 1888 and is buried in the family tomb in St Peter and St Paul's church Swanscombe.

❏ ❏ ❏

When a child in Chatham, Charles Dickens and his father John occasionally visited Higham on the Rochester to Gravesend road. In doing so they passed the red brick Gad's Hill Place, a large country house, and his father would turn to Charles and tell him that if he worked hard one day he might own a house similar to it. In 1856, by now a famous author, he bought it for £1,790.

'At the present moment I am on my little Kentish freehold looking on as pretty a view out of my study window as you will find in a long day's English ride,' he wrote to a friend. 'Cobham woods and park are behind the house, the distant Thames in front, the Medway with Rochester and its old castle and cathedral on one side. The whole stupendous property is on the old Dover Road'.

❏ ❏ ❏

On his way between two of his principal places of call, Kipps, the hero of H G Wells' novel of that name, set in Folkestone, would go:

. . . along the Leas to the lift, watch the lift up and down twice, but no longer because that wouldn't do, back along the Leas, watch the harbour for a short time and then round by the churchyard and so (hurrying) into Church Street and Rendezvous Street . . .

The 'most beautiful castle in Britain' appears to float in a lake among fields and trees south of Hollingbourne, near Maidstone. Leeds Castle was built

on islands in the River Len, which forms a moat around it, and was the favourite country retreat of Edward I's queen, Eleanor of Castile, and Catherine de Valois, widow of Henry V.

The castle was given to the nation in 1976 by its last private owner, Lady Olive Baillie. Visitors can see the suite of rooms used by the medieval queens, set out as they would have been in the fifteenth century and walk through HenryVIII's 75ft long banqueting hall. There is also a dog collar museum, its earliest exhibits dating back to the days of Queen Anne.

In 1821 George IV took ship to and from Ramsgate to visit his relations in Hanover. The citizens were so grateful for this 'gracious condescension' towards their town that they raised an obelisk upon the spot the monarch placed his gouty foot when he stepped ashore. The inscription on it reads:

TO GEORGE THE FOURTH, KING OF GREAT BRITAIN AND IRELAND THE INHABITANTS AND VISITORS OF RAMSGATE AND THE DIRECTORS AND TRUSTEES OF THE HARBOUR HAVE ERECTED THIS OBELISK AS A GRATEFUL RECORD OF HIS MAJESTY'S GRACIOUS CONDESCENSION IN SELECTING THIS PORT FOR HIS EMBARKATION ON THE 25TH SEPTEMBER IN PROGRESS TO HIS KINGDOM OF HANOVER AND HIS HAPPY RETURN ON THE 8TH NOVEMBER 1821

Kent and the Natural World

There have been sheep on Romney Marsh since 700 AD when they were kept for their wool and milk.

Kent historian, Richard Kilburne, writing in 1659, had this fine fisherman's tale to tell:

A monstrous fish in July, 1574, shot himself on shore near Broadstairs, when for want of water he died the next day. While he died he roared so loud the noise could be heard a mile away. No one would approach him; the boldest fisherman was scared. His length was 22 feet, the nether jaw opening 12 feet. One of his eyes was more than a cart and six horses could draw and a man stood upright in tbe place from where the eye was taken. Three men stood upright in the mouth; a man could creep into his nostrils; his tongue was 15 feet long.

✻ ✻ ✻

The Kentish Glory is a moth, with several brown shades on fore and hind wings, marked also with white patches and black zig-zag lines and, in particular, with a black mark on each fore wing. The green caterpillars feed on birch leaves. Formerly it was common in certain localities in Kent, hence its name, and also in Sussex,

Berkshire and Worcestershire. In the 1870s it was so prolific that a hundred males were caught by a collector in one day. Now it is only found in birch woods in Scotland.

❀ ❀ ❀

Twelve Marsh Frogs, *Rana ridibunda,* were brought in 1935 from Debrecen in Hungary by Mr E P Smith and put in the pond in his garden at Stone-in-Oxney. They settled down and the population expanded into the numerous dykes nearby and are now firmly established in Romney Marsh, Walland Marsh and the adjacent area.

The Marsh Frog is larger than the native Common Frog. The female is up to 5 inches (128mm) long, the male 3fi inches (90mm) and they are greyish-brown to uniform light green or black-spotted green in colour.

It has received a mixed reception from local residents because in the breeding season the very vocal males keep up a chorus of spasmodic croaking throughout the night, keeping people living up to half-a-mile away awake.

Being able to supply their especial soil preference Kent has more wild orchids in its flora than any other county. Some are rare, even in Kent, others locally common.

They include the Early Purple, Bird's Nest, Green Man, Frog, Lizard,Broad-leaved Helleborine, White Helleborine, Twayblade, Bee, Fly, Lady or Dark-winged, Autumn Ladies Tresses, Green-winged, Spotted, Burnt or Dwarf, Pyramidal, Fragrant, Early Spider, Late Spider, Monkey and Greater Butterfly.

Many of the orchids, like the Bee Orchid pictured left, were named after creatures they were thought to resemble.

In his *History and Antiquities of the Isle of Thanet in Kent,* 1736, the Reverend John Lewis mentions an order ' . . . to forbid and restrain the burning or taking up of any sea oare within the Isle of Thanet'. This is probably a reference in part to Queen Elisabeth I who, in 1573, journeyed in Kent and was not always pleased with what she saw. She reputedly banned the burning of seaweed at Oare and also on the Thanet coast because of fears that smoke from it could damage the health of people in the area.

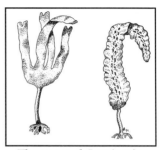

The oarweed, Laminaria Digitata and Laminaria Saccharina

The ash of the oarweed, as it came to be known, was used in soap making and as a fertiliser.

When the Channel Tunnel was excavated there was a problem – what to do with the seven million cubic metres of soft grey chalk marl removed. Some went to France but nearly five million cubic metres was used to create the open site near the base of the famous White Cliffs known as Samphire Hoe. The marl was heaped onto the site, then landscaped, water pools made for seabirds, and seeds of wild flowers and grasses, suitable for the conditions, sown. Gradually the plants have colonised the area, and have encouraged insects and birds to do so.

Samphire Hoe is between Folkestone and Dover and reached via a cliff tunnel. It is open daily to dusk for walkers, cyclists and wheelchair users, without charge except for car parking. The further a visitor gets from the car park the more naturally wild the site, with its impressive backcloth of Shakespeare Cliff, becomes.

It was named Samphire Hoe as samphire, *Crithmum maritimum,* which has edible, thick, fleshy bluish-green leaves and stems and white flowers, grows on the Hoe and cliffs. In the past it was gathered in quantity and sent to London's markets.

Thomas Fuller, author of *Worthies of England*, published in the 1640s, declared that the cattle and poultry of Kent were ' the largest in the land.' He instanced:

a giant ox, fed on the Romney marsh, that was some six years since been seen in London, so high that one of ordinary stature could hardly reach the top of his back.

This may have been the same animal mentioned by John Evelyn in his Diary on 29 April 1649:

I saw in London a huge ox bred in Kent 17 feet in length and much higher than I could reach.

❊ ❊ ❊

Bewl Water, a mile south of Lamberhurst, is the largest lake in south-east England. It is one of the country's leading fly fisheries and is stocked with 55,000 trout annually.

The reservoir was created in 1975 by damming the river Bewl, a tributary of the Medway, and flooding a valley. It covers 770 acres and it takes four to five hours to walk the 13 miles water route through the woodland

and meadows that surround it. It is quicker on horseback – or by mountain bike, which can be hired from there.

'All the hops are gathered, but the oasts are still busy and a piercing fragrance fills the sharp moving air. If you walk in the woods after sunset you will meet the labourers making their way back to Rough Common or Blean, carrying tools and faggots and bags of apples, wildish-looking bearded men with bright eyes. Tbe hop wagons go creaking by, day and night and the plough is busy on all the sloping cornfields by Petite France and Densted.'

Mrs Mary Sybilla Holland, to her sister, Cathy, in the autumn of 1888, from Harbledown Lodge, Upper Harbledown, bought by her husband, a Canon of Canterbury Cathedral, in 1887.

Kent and Religion

The cross that marks the site of the church of the vanished village of Orgarswick.

On Romney Marsh there are several sites or remains of churches built to serve a small local population and abandoned when the community was

either decimated by sickness, such as the Black Death, or it became too difficult to gain a living from the land. Eventually the churches fell into ruin or disappeared completely.

One that survived as a ruin is at Eastbridge, part of the tower and some fragmented sections of the church walls are alongside the Dymchurch to Bonnington road near Eastbridge House. At Orgarswick, near Dymchurch. a cross erected in 1932, marks the site of the church that served the vanished village which, in the 1801 census, had a population of six. Other examples are at Hope All Saints, Blackmanstone and Midley.

Remains of Eastbridge church.

The King's School, Canterbury, had its beginnings as a school for boys founded about 600 AD shortly after Saint Augustine and his followers landed at Ebbsfleet,Thanet. The reasoning was that if future generations were to understand Augustine's teachings and take part in the new worship it was necessary for them to learn Latin. So the school was founded in what was to become St Alphege parish where it is still.

On the creation of a bishopric of Rochester in 604 a boys' grammar school was also founded there, based on the Canterbury model. In 1541, after Christ Church monastery had been dissolved, Henry VIII re-founded the school but under the control of the Dean and Chapter of Canterbury cathedral. It was not until the late seventeenth century, however, that it became known as the King's School. From these origins it is reputed to be the oldest boys' school in England. Old boys include Christopher Marlowe, John Tradescant, William Harvey, Hugh Walpole and Somerset Maugham.

There are numerous graffiti scratchings in Canterbury cathedral, some of them dating from the twelfth century. One, in the entrance to the eastern crypt, is of a knight on horseback. On the south-west wall of the crypt is an incised illustration dating from the early thirteenth century and showing Christ in Majesty, seated among the symbols of the Four Evangelists.

Behind a buttress on the north side of the Trinity Chapel is a scratching showing the Last Supper with John resting his head on Christ's bosom. It is thought that some of these incised outlines were the preparation work for paintings that were not, in the end, executed.

There is some curious Kentish ironwork on the south door of All Saints church, Staplehurst. It is probably twelfth century and may relate the Viking legend of Ragnarok, the Twilight of the Gods, for its motifs include a dragon, snakes, fishes, a Viking ship, a ship's figurehead and crosses.

Around the chancel arch and facing the nave of Holy Cross church, Hoath two miles north east of Grove Ferry, is the declaration, in red and blue capital letters:

THIS IS THE HOUSE OF GOD
THIS IS THE GATE OF HEAVEN.

Tbe style of the lettering suggests that it was a Victorian addition.

A sculptured head, perhaps of Christ, looks down from a chancel wall to face the congregation but undoubtedly the greatest treasure of the church is a rare palimpsest brass to Anthony Maycot and his wife. It is dated 1532.

Set in the flint wall that encloses the Kent War Memorial Garden in the precincts of Canterbury cathedral is an oblong stone, inscribed with the double Cross of Ypres, brought from the ruins of the Cloth Hall at Ypres, which was destroyed by artillery fire and bombing in the First World War.

The Sailors church, more usually known as the Little Church by the Sea, is on the quayside of Ramsgate harbour, close to the West Pier. It was built and

opened in 1878 as part of the Sailors Home and Harbour Mission, founded by the Reverend Eustace Brenan. The mission also accommodated, on its upper floor, the smack boys who helped to crew fishing smacks in the nineteenth century.

In 1881 a separate Home for Smack Boys was built adjoining the church and the vacated rooms above the mission were used to shelter shipwrecked

The Sailors' church and, on the right, the Smack Boys' Home.

seafarers. Over the years more than 3,300 of them were cared for there.

In the reign of Roman Catholic Queen Mary forty-one Protestants – thirty men, eleven women – were burnt at the stake in Canterbury for refusing to renounce their faith. On the site, then a field and now a small public garden in a road off Wincheap, aptly named Martyrs Field Road, stands the Martyrs' Memorial, a grey Cornish granite column surmounted by a Canterbury Cross, on a base of the same rock. The site was given, the surrounding ground purchased and the monument erected by public subscription.

The memorial bears the inscription:

IN MEMORY OF FORTY ONE KENTISH MARTYRS WHO WERE BURNT AT THE STAKE ON THIS SPOT IN THE REIGN OF QUEEN MARY 1555-1558. FOR THEMSELVES THEY EARNED THE MARTYRS CROWN. BY THEIR HEROIC FIDELITY THEY HELPED TO SECURE FOR SUCCEEDING GENERATIONS THE PRICELESS BLESSING OF RELIGIOUS FREEDOM.

Among the martyrs whose names are inscribed on the memorial are John Bland, vicar of Adisham and John Frankesh, vicar of Rolvenden.

According to popular belief the Devil is cloven-hoofed. Not true. At Newington-by-Sittingbourne is evidence that he wears size 15 boots. Near the gate to St Mary's church is a 3½ft high, round-topped, upright sarsen stone. Low down on one side is the unmistakable shape of a bootprint. The sole is 10 inches long and 5 inches wide, the heel 5inches by 4 inches.

Legend relates that, annoyed with the ringing of the church bells, the Devil stole them and put them in a sack which he slung over his shoulder. Then he saw the vicar approaching and he leapt from the tower. Where one foot landed the earth became rock beneath it, capturing his bootprint and causing Old Nick to overbalance. He dropped the sack and the bells rolled down the lane and into a stream – to be lost forever.

62

Kent Food and Drink

Kent is a cultivated cherry growing county, and also has both species of wild cherry, so it is to be expected that there are numerous local recipes for cherry wines and brandies, tarts, puddings, jams and preserves.

In the old days Kentish Cherry Beer was traditionally drunk at Easter while eating Kentish Pudding Pies. To make it 3 lbs of demerara sugar, 3 lbs of Morello cherries and 1 quart of draught beer were needed.

The cherries were first pricked with a fork to release their juice, then put into a large stone jar with the sugar and stirred with a wooden spoon. When thoroughly mixed the beer was poured in and the contents of the jar stirred again. The mixture was then left to stand for six months before the liquid was drawn off, bottled and kept for a further six months to mature.

⌛ ⌛ ⌛

In former days the young shoots of the wild hop were sought in springtime to be boiled and eaten as asparagus. In 1892 a Mr Snelling took out a patent for Hop Tea when he found that an infusion of the hop cone petals tasted, so he claimed, like certain brands of Indian tea. He formed the Hop

Tea Company, buying hops while green from the growers. They were taken to the company's Maidstone factory and dried according to his 'formula'. The petals were then separated and rolled through his patented tea rolling machine before being fermented, and again dried with hot air, until they looked like the leaves of Indian tea. The hop 'tea' was then taken to the company's London factory to be blended. According to advertisements for Snelling's Patent Tea great care was taken with the blend-ing for it was in the drying of the hop petals that the volatile oil in them was developed to impart the hop tea's special aroma.

Initially there was a demand for Hop Tea, particularly from sufferers from dyspepsia who could not drink ordinary tea. However, the demand soon declined and the company closed.

⌛   ⌛   ⌛

The old country recipe for Kentish Well Pudding has no connection with a well of water. The ingredients required for it are 1lb of flour, 6 ounces of suet, 6 ounces of currants, ½lb of fresh butter, 2 tablespoonfuls of moist sugar and a little baking powder.

Make a suet crust with the flour, suet and currants and roll out to the thickness of about an inch. Cut the pastry into a circle, retaining the trimmings for the top, and line a greased pudding basin with it. Place the butter in the well and fill it up with the sugar. Roll out the remaining pastry, cut into a circle and place on top, joining the edges well. Cover with a greased paper or a pudding cloth and steam for three to four hours.

⧗　⧗　⧗

'How do you do, Mrs Howard? That is all I have to say, if my brain could have produced anything sooner you should have heard from me. This afternoon I am taken with a fit of writing, but as to matter, I have nothing better to entertain you with but to tell you news of my farm. I therefore give you the following list of the stock of eatables I am fatting for my private tooth.

It is well known to the whole County of Kent that I have four fat calves, two fat hogs, twelve promising black pigs, four white sows big with child, for whom I have great compassion, two young chickens, three fine geese sitting with thirteen eggs under each (several being duck eggs), carp in plenty, beef and mutton at very reasonable rates.

Now, Mrs Howard, if you have a mind to stick your knife in anything I have named, say so. Nothing has happened here since I came worth mentioning in history, but a bloody retaliation committed on the body of an owl that destroyed our pigeons.'

This original and entertaining invitation to a meal was in a letter to a friend from Mary Bellenden of Combe Bank, Sundridge, in 1723.

⏳   ⏳   ⏳

'The polite palate professes a distaste for Romney Marsh mutton as too coarse. With the craze for small mutton which became universal in the Eighties, large mutton fell out of demand. The local gourmet, however, will tell you that Marsh mutton in summer and autumn is the primest of meats.'

A G Bradley in An Old Gate of England, *published in 1917.*

⧗   ⧗   ⧗

The ingredients of what was presumably a traditional Kentish stew with which Charles Dickens was familiar are itemised in *The Old Curiosity Shop.*

'It's a stew of tripe' said the landlord smacking his lips, 'and cowheel', smacking them again, 'and bacon', smacking them once more, 'and steak', smacking them for the fourth time, 'and peas, cauliflower, new potatoes, and sparrow grass, (asparagus) all worked up together in one delicious gravy.'

⧗   ⧗   ⧗

The Kentish saying 'as sure as there's a dog in Dover' means something is really certain and as definite as the fact that large numbers of 'dogs' (dogfish) used to be landed at Dover.

Kent's fish and chip shops today still use Huss, Bull Huss, Robin Huss, Rock Salmon and Gurnet as names for this fish but the correct name is Dogfish and the variety is usually the Lesser Spotted.

⧗　⧗　⧗

The River Stour at Fordwich had 'trouts differing from all others in many considerables, notably largeness, in cunning and flesh whiteness.' Izaak Walton, in the *Compleat Angler,* first published in 1653, refers to it:

. . . .a Fordidge trout . . . is accounted the rarest of fish, many of them near the bigness of a salmon but known by their different colour and in their best season they cut very white.

⧗　⧗　⧗

John Sills, a grocer of Ashford, kept a diary entitled *Memorandums of Occurances*, which included this complaint about his dissatisfaction with a meal he had in Sandgate:

On Thursday, 8th August, 1820, myself, Margaret Sills and William Morley went in my chaise to Sandgate . . . we dined there, us three, off from a Lamb chop, a few Potatoes and a few French Beans. It was cooked well, but the chops were brought in very sparingly. I should think not about 1½ or a short 2 lbs. When we rang the bell they was going to take the dish away and put on the Cheese, but I told them we wanted another chop, so after a while they brought us three more small chops. Our bill amounted to nine shillings, sixpence for beer and one shillingworth of brandy and water. No tart. No pudding. A very dear House.

Kent Sport and Leisure

Tonbridge cricket ground.

Cricket has been played in Kent since 1705. An advertisement appeared on 27 July that year announcing that a 'match of cricket' between '11 gentlemen of the west part of the county of Kent against as many of Chatham for 11 guineas a man, at Malling' was to be held on 5 August.

In 1709 the same journal, *The Postman,* printed a report of a game played between Kent and Surrey for £50. The two sides were not chosen from across the counties – the match was between a team from Dartford and a team from somewhere in Surrey. In 1734 Kent beat Sussex at Sevenoaks with Lord Sackville and Lord Middlesex in the Kent team.

Wagers were laid on the result of almost every game. When Kent, with Lord Middlesex again in the side, played against a Middlesex team raised by the Prince of Wales in 1735 it was a £1,000-a-side match. Kent won.

After beating an All-England side in 1739 Kent was credited as being 'the unconquerable county.' A Kent county club was founded at Town Malling in 1836 but had little success in spite of the introduction, six years later, of Canterbury's famous Cricket Week. Another, more firmly-based, county club was established at Maidstone in 1858, with the sixth Earl of Darnley of Cobham Hall as its first president. In 1870 this club amalgamated with the Beverley Cricket Club, Canterbury and the Kent County Cricket Club came into being.

One of the club's best periods was from 1967 to 1978 when Kent won the Championship twice, shared it once, three times won the John Player League, won the Benson and Hedges Cup three times and won the Gillette Cup twice. In 2001 the county won the Norwich Union National League Trophy and great achievements are expected from the present young Kent team in the future.

Credited with being the first maker of cricket bats is William Pett (1710-1786) who lived at Sevenoaks where his family owned property. He realised that the sport was rapidly increasing in popularity throughout southern England and seized the opportunity to supply the bats needed by players. At first his bats were curved, like the one pictured left, but later on he made them with straight blades, although some examples were wider at the bottom than at the top.

The Vine, Sevenoaks, is believed to be the oldest cricket ground in Kent. The first recorded match there was between Kent and Sussex in 1734 and it is virtually certain that Pett supplied the bats. He had a shop in Sevenoaks High Street but also sold bats through toy shops in towns and cities in the south. They varied in price from half a crown (12½p) to four shillings (20p) and four shillings and sixpence (22½p). In the archives at Knole there is an account dated 20 June, 1766 sent by Pett to the 3rd Duke of Dorset for 'eleven cricket batts, £1.7s.6d.'

A genuine Pett bat is stamped 'PETT 7OAKS KENT'.

The 'Lion of Kent', 18 to 20 stone 6ft tall Alfred Mynn, was a member of the county side for 25 years from 1834, and played in 99 matches. It was said of him:

His delivery was noble, walking majestically up to the crease, though when he first began he used to advance with a run. His bowling was very fast and ripping-round-armed and of a good length.

When he died Mynn was accorded military honours at his funeral. His headstone in St Mary's churchyard, Thurnham. records that 400 people united to erect it and to found, in his honour, the Mynn Memorial Benevolent Institution for Kent cricketers with:

£121 16s 0d invested in India five per cent stocks to benefit in perpetuity the above-named charity.

On one occasion, before leg pads were introduced, Mynn played right through an innings, scoring 146 runs, with one leg so badly injured by rival bowling that at the end of the game he had to be laid flat on top of a coach to be taken to hospital.

On the north side of St. Vincent's church, Littlebourne, is the table tomb of 'sportsman' Henry Denne, who died in 1822. Between 1770 and 1809 he shot 2,322 partridges, 753 pheasants, 2,079 hares, 3,764 rabbits, 1,682 woodcock, 2,552 snipe, 600 wildfowl, 700 landrail, and two eagles.

In his will he asked that a perched black eagle, the one he shot in 1770, be carved in a cartouche at one end of his tomb, and the second eagle, that he shot in 1797, be carved in a cartouche at the other end – as they are.

Bat and Trap is an ancient Kentish game, played on a 21-yard long grass pitch, but of any width. At one end of the pitch is the trap, the other end being the bowling end with two posts 12½ feet apart. The trap has a pivoted bar and at its front a depression for the solid rubber ball. The batsman puts the ball in the depression then strikes the rear end of the bar with his bat. This flings the ball in the air and the batsman tries to hit it down the pitch and between the posts with his wooden bat, which is 5½ inches wide and 8inches long. If he fails or is caught he is out. In front of the trap is a 5 inch square, white flap with a black centre 2¼ inches in diameter. The flap is hinged and drops when hit by the ball thrown from the bowling end. If the returned ball, when thrown at it, fails to knock down the flap or 'take his trap' the batsman scores a run although he does not have to run down the pitch. A batsman's score is the number of times the opposing team throws at and misses his trap. There are eight in a side, each member of the 'in' team taking a turn while the 'out' or opposing team stand between the other end posts.

Behind the batsman and the trap is anything that will act as a barrier to stop the ball going too far such as a fence, wall, hedge, or netting. A game consists of three innings by each side; a match is of three games. As the batsman scores a run for every miss and does no actual running there is no fielding and the game is a leisurely one.

Bat and Trap is still played in East Kent, either as sides of men, and women too, taking part in a league against rivals, or just as an attraction at a village pub.

The first rules for lawn tennis were drawn up by Sir William Hart Dyke and some friends when sitting on the lawn at his home, Lullingstone Castle, near Eynsford,in 1875. The game was intended to be a simplified outdoor version of real tennis, using a net, but no walls. They played a game, but not having a net they used a ladder supported on two barrels instead.

The game of goal-running is described by F J Harvey Darton in *A Parcel of Kent*, published in 1924:

> All that is wanted for a goal-running match is a field (preferably near an inn; it is a game which breeds a very healthy and genuine thirst), an

emblematical standard for each side, four umpires, two standard-bearers and a number of men, limited only when great issues are at stake, divisible by two.

The game, which survived into the 1920s, was in principle a form of tag, with two teams of 22 men running in turn around a *gaule* (or goal) post – hence the name. Players wore a vest and running shorts and plimsolls or just socks or were barefooted. The team achieving the highest total of strokes or points by touching their rival players was the winner.

Sandwich in medieval times was the principal and one of the most prosperous coastal ports of England, but gradually the sea receded leaving an expanse of sand in Sandwich Bay. Although the silting sand finished Sandwich as a port it later on brought prosperity in another form to the town. It became, and still is, a noted golfing centre.

An expatriate Scotman, Ian Purves, saw the bay area as an ideal situation for a first class golf course. In 1887 he founded the Royal St George's Club and in 1905 the Prince's Club was founded. They were both championship courses from the start and filled the need for full-length sand courses in this part of England.

Walter Jerrold, writing in his *Highways and Byways in Kent* in 1907, said of this former port and its enthusiasm for golf:

On approaching Sandwich from the north the way in which all sorts and conditions of people play the great game is strikingly manifest. Girls not yet in their teens are playing here; there is a burly drayman, it is the dinner hour, handling his iron with vigour and precision. We might be in the town of St Andrews by the way in which all ages and all classes follow the game.

The Tom Thumb Theatre on Eastern Esplanade, Cliftonville is the smallest theatre in Kent and can claim to have the smallest stage of any public theatre in Britain – it measures a mere 7ft by 10ft. The building was formerly a coach-house, then a two-car garage, and it was near-derelict when it was sold to theatrical agent Lesley Parr-Byrne, and her actress daughter, Sarah, in 1984. Lesley had always wanted her own theatre and spent £30,000 converting the building into a 58-seat red and gold Victorian-style theatre in miniature. The dressing room is still, at present, a beach chalet in the garden.

The theatre is open from Easter to October, and for a pantomime at Christmas. The programmes include drama, comedy, period pieces, music hall – all performed by professional actors and actresses more for the fun of it than for petrol and expenses.

The theatre is licensed for weddings and couples can be married on its stage while guests watch the proceedings from the auditorium.

🏴 🏴 🏴

A stable in Margate was converted into a playhouse in 1779 at a cost of £200 by sea captain Charles Mate, who was interested in acting and the stage. In 1786 he obtained a royal charter from George III and moved his playhouse to its present site where, on 27 June 1787, it opened as the Theatre Royal. One of the first to perform there was Mrs Sarah Siddons and a later attraction was General Tom Thumb – the American midget Charles Sherwood Stratton, who was only 40 inches (102cm) tall.

The Theatre Royal has in its time been a furniture warehouse containing some 20,000 Government-property beds; a cinema; a venue for all-in wrestling; and a bingo hall. It is now once again a successful theatre.

Kent at Christmas

Best Christmas and New Year Wishes

In Kent preparations for the Christmas festivities started on the twenty-fifth Sunday after Trinity. The Sunday nearest to St Andrew's Day, 30 November, was known as Stir Up Sunday, so-named because the Collect for that day is:

> Stir up, we beseech Thee, O Lord, the wills of
> Thy faithful people
> that they plenteously bringing forth the fruit of
> good works,
> may of Thee be plenteously rewarded.

Housewives and cooks would hurry home from church and gather together all the ingredients for the Christmas pudding. Everyone in the household had at least one stir of the pudding mixture, traditionally with a wood spoon. First to stir would be mother, then father, followed by the children in descending ages, then any other members of the household. It was thought important to stir sunwise, from east to west, following the course of the sun which was vital for ripening the corn. The stirring was done silently, and a secret wish was made. In some families the pudding was stirred three times for luck, and three wishes were made but only one would be granted.

❋ ❋ ❋

A Maidstone nurseryman, George Bunyard, introduced the dessert apple Christmas Pearmain in 1893. It is a sweet, russet variety and at its best to eat from mid-December onwards. In 1871 Bunyard introduced the Gascoynes Scarlet which had been developed by a Mr Gascoyne at Sittingbourne. This dessert apple when ripe has a bright red flush over a pale greenish-cream and finally becomes red and cream. In Victorian times it was often grown mainly as a decoration to be displayed on a plate in homes, churches and inns at Christmas.

❋ ❋ ❋

In the countryside of Kent, particularly in the Romney Marsh area, flead cakes were eaten for breakfast, and at tea time, on Christmas Day. These cakes, the basic ingredient of which is the fat enveloping a pig's kidneys, were also eaten throughout the year.

The flead, or fleed, had to be chopped, chopped and chopped again with a hot meat chopper, the blade of which was repeatedly dipped into a jug of near-boiling water. When the flead had reached the consistency of lard it was mixed with flour, egg, salt and cold water and the resulting dough rolled out and cut into small rounds, brushed with beaten egg and baked until golden brown. They were eaten piping hot.

❄ ❄ ❄

Eltham Palace was formerly in Kent and not part of Greater London and in this royal residence English kings from Edward II to Henry VIII liked to celebrate Christmas, often on a lavish scale. When Edward IV feasted 2,000 guests at Eltham in 1482, the amount of food required was enormous - 1,000 sheep, 300 calves, 2,000 kids, 6 bulls, 800 pigs, 12 porpoises and seals, 2,000 swans, 1,000 geese, 2,000 capons, 1,200 plovers, 2,400 quails, 400 peacocks, 200 cranes, 4,000 bitterns, 200 herons, 1,000 curlews, 4,000 dishes of jelly, 2,000 hot custards, 1,000 cold venison pastries, 1,500 hot venison pastries, plenty of spices, sugared delicacies and wafers.

❄ ❄ ❄

When he was the editor of *Household Words* in the 1850s Charles Dickens also wrote some of the articles. In one he gave this description of a well decorated Christmas tree:

> It was brilliantly lighted by a multitude of little tapers and everywhere sparkled and glittered with bright objects. There were rosy-cheeke dolls hiding behind the green leaves and there were real watches (with moveable hands at least) dangling from innumerable twigs. There were French-polished tables, chairs, bedsteads, wardrobes, eight-

day clocks and various other articles of domestic furniture . . . there were jolly, broadfaced little men. . . their heads took off and showed them full of sugar plums; there were fiddles and drums, there were tambourines, books, workboxes, paintboxes, sweetmeat boxes, peepshow boxes, and all kinds of boxes; there were trinkets for the elder girls, far brighter than any grown-up gold and jewels; there were baskets and pincushions in all devices; there were guns, swords, banners; there were witches in enchanted rings of pasteboard; there were teetotums, humming tops, needle-cases, penwipers, smelling bottles, conversation cards, bouquet holders; real fruit, made artificially dazzling with goldleaf; imitation apples, pears and walnuts, crammed with surprises; in short, as a pretty child before me delightedly whispered to another friend, 'There was everything and more'.

❄ ❄ ❄

One of the few examples of a Christmas charity in Kent church benefactions, the majority being for Easter, is the Bedingfield Charity at Dymchurch.

It was founded by Captain Timothy Bedingfield (l643-1693) who is believed to be buried in the old churchyard, and was a gift of:

5/- a peece unto two poor women of the parish to be paid on 25th December after they have received the Sacrament.

He also initiated a local educational scheme for 'poor male children' by a gift of land at Woodchurch and Liming – details of which are given on his memorial tablet on the nave wall in St Peter's church. A Bedingfield scholarship scheme is still in existence.

❊ ❊ ❊

There is an East Kent saying: 'if ye the Hooden Horse do feed, throughout the year ye shall not need.'

The horse was part of the Hoodening custom, possibly of pagan origin, which took place in various parts of Kent at Christmas, and at spring and autumn hop festivals. The ceremony was witnessed at the turn of the century by Joseph Wright and he described it in his *English Dialect Dictionary* of 1902:

We were warned of the arrival of this creature by a very loud clapping noise and on rushing to the street door saw a horse's head, supported on a pole by a man in a crawling position to resemble an animal and covered in the front by a coarse cloth . . . the clapping, caused by the opening and shutting of the mouth, continued until the creature, having been satisfied with money, was driven away.

The Hooden Horse consisted of a carved wooden head of a horse fixed to a long pole straddled by a man covered with a sheet or horse blanket. The head was decorated with colourful rosettes and ribbons, brass-headed nails formed its teeth, it had painted or coloured glass eyes, and the lower jaw was hinged and could be opened and closed vigorously to make a loud clapping sound by the man beneath the sheet pulling on a cord attached to it.

Also taking part in this colourful fund-raising ritual was the Waggoner, who led the horse by a bridle,

Molly, or the Old Woman with a broom, the Squire, a Fool, and sometimes a fiddler.

The custom almost died out but in recent years has been enthusiastically revived in conjunction with teams of Morris dancers, carol singers and handbell ringers.

❄ ❄ ❄

YE OLDE VILLAGE OF RENHAM

This toast to the New Year, which encapsulates the history of Kent, was written by W J Smith who, in the 1940s, was headmaster of the boys' section of Rainham Senior School.

To the Ancient Man, who, dressed in woad and carrying a club, pushed his way through the forest and gazed on the coastal marshes.

To the North Sea warrior who pushed up Renham Creek at high tide and held his own against the Stone Age and the Bronze.

To the Roman centurion in charge of this section of the Road who built his villa nearby.

To the Saxon chief who cleared the land and settled here.

To the Christiasn missionary who raised his Cross on the tribal clearing.

To the men of Renham who defied the heathen Danes.

To those who journeyed to Swanscombe and won freedom for their children from the Conqueror's Law.

To the De Crevequer who built his church in thanksgiving.

To the monks of Leeds who beautified the site with a worthier building.

To the Lords of the Manor who rebuilt the nave.

To the holder of the compasses that described the circle for the first Consecration Cross.

To the craftsmen who made the old chest when the Black Prince was a boy.

To the men of Renham who drew bowstrings at Crecy and Poitiers.

To the first Renham Member of Parliament.

To the builders of the noble tower.

To those who hobnobbed with the boy Drake off Renham Creek.

To him who kindled the Beacon turret fire when the Armada sailed up the Channel.

To the man who pulled the bell and the woman who screamed with fear as she snatched up her child.

To the Fire Brigade who raced the fire hook from the church and dragged off the burning thatch.

To him who planted the hop and cherry and brewed good beer.

To the enlightened and brave who helped Renham* to Protestantism.

To the Earl of Thanet who suffered for loyalty to his king.

To the frightened women and children when the Dutch sailed up the Medway.

To the old stage coachman who joyed to see upstanding the old church tower.

To the potters and the brickmakers.

To the Volunteers who prepared a warm welcome for Napoleon.

To the lads of the village who made the great sacrifice in the Great War.

To the present generation that tries to be worthy of the past.

To the future generations that shall accomplish all that we would have done.

*An alternative spelling of Rainham

BIBLIOGRAPHY

Bignell, Alan. *The Kent Village Book*, Countryide Books 1986

Braddock, Joseph. *Footpaths of the Kent-Sussex Border,* Chaterson 1947

Brewster, Eddie. *Theatre Royal History*. Friends of the Theatre Royal newsletters, 1996-1997

Croydon, B. *Early Birds – A Short History of How Flight came to Sheppey,* Sheppey Heritage Trust

Field, Barnett. *The Hooden Horse of East Kent,* Folklore, Vol 78 1967

Fielding, C H. *Memories of Malling and its Valley,* Henry Oliver 1893

Jessup, Ronald F. *Kent – The Little Guide*, Methuen/Batsford 1950

Lane, Anthony. *Maritime Kent*, Tempus 2000

Lapthorne, William H. *A Broad Place,* and *Historic Broadstairs,* Thanet Antiquarian Book Club 1980

Moore, Dudley. *The History of Kent County Cricket Club*, Christopher Helm 1989

Newman, John. *West Kent and the Weald*, Penguin 1969

Osbourne, Peter, edit. *Harbledown Heritage,* Harbledown Conservation Association 2000

A Short History of the Acquisition and Restoration of Royal Terrace Pier by Pilots, 1893

MAGAZINES
Pre-war and post-war editions of *The Kent Journal* and the *Kent and Sussex Journal*

PICTURE CREDITS

With the exception of the photograph by Diana Bailey of Rock Villa, Tunbridge Wells on page 38 and the Royal Terrace Pier on page 40, all photographs are by the author or from his collection.

ACKNOWLEDGEMENTS

The author wishes to thank, for help generously given, Kate Clifford, Local Studies Librarian, Gravesend; the Reference Library staff, Sevenoaks Library; Wendy Page, Bewl Water, Lamberhurst; Dr Joan Basden, Bonnyrigg; and Tony Turner.

Special thanks to Diana M Bailey, Tunbridge Wells, for her useful advice and assistance with research in the preparation of this book.